Blessons for Living
The BEST of BEING

Written By: Elena M. Neely
Illustrated by: Terry Did'Um

Blessons for Living: The BEST of BEING

ISBN 978-0-578-77951-5

Copyright © Elena M. Neely

Published by Blessons For Living, LLC
www.blessonsforliving.com

Illustrated by: Terry Did'Um

Printed in the United States of America © 2020 All rights reserved.
No part of this book may be reproduced or copied in any form without written permission from the author.

Dedication

I dedicate this book to God, who inspires the Blessons for Living project and blesses those engaged in bringing it to life. To my beautiful Mom, Jacquie, who gave me life and who passed a few days before the launch of the first book, "Blessons For Living, Planting Seeds of Greatness."

To my daughter, Amaya, who is living proof that reading at a young age has benefits for years to come. Finally, I dedicate this book to every person reading it right now. This moment in time is precious and predestined. I wish for you and your family an extraordinary future.

Acknowledgments

I'd like to thank my dear friends Winsome Humphrey and Jerome White for their spiritual advisement, prayers, wise counsel and love. I would like to acknowledge Ann Kendricks, Certified Life Strategies Coach of *Amazing You!* Ann is a steady guide, a focused arrow to guide me to the completion of my life objectives. I'd like to acknowledge my amazing illustrator, Terry Did'Um Bolen, whose illustrations bring words to life to fully engage young readers. Much appreciation to Chris Jones, a man who sincerely cares about our youth and who contributed the book's Foreword. Finally, to my daughter Amaya Neely, who inspires me to be bold in love.

Introduction

Blessons for Living, The BEST of BEING! Every person in the world has 24 hours in a day to choose how they will live. They get to choose how they will spend their time, what choices they will make and what attitudes they will have. The actions a person takes and every choice that they make adds to the person that they are and who they will become. As you may have heard, actions become habits. Habits become character and character becomes your destiny. This second book in the Blessons for Living series is about the BEST of BEING!

Blessons are lessons shared. They don't become blessings until they are shared. That is why the "Blessons For Living" book series was created, to share life's most important lessons with the youngest possible recipient. The first book, "Blessons for Living, Planting Seeds of Greatness," focused on the most basic lessons, like Sleeping, Learning, Loving Yourself, and the power of The Mind. This book, "The BEST of BEING," focuses on what we do in moments of time. Will you Be Helpful, Be Kind, Be Brave, Be Curious? Be a Friend, Be Happy? This book highlights the BEST of BEING. Sharing these jewels with your young ones is beautiful and necessary.

Please share this book with your loved ones, enjoy reading it with them or just enjoy reading it yourself. I hope this book blesses you as much as it blessed me to write it.

Foreword by
Chris Jones, Author
10 Ways Teenagers Mess Up Their Options: Turn it Around
National Youth Speaker

When I initially met the book's author Elena Neely about 10 years ago, I sensed that she was going to be someone who would make a difference. The fact that she has become a children's book author is of no surprise to me. She is extremely articulate, animated and has the ability to capture a person's attention in conversation or the written word.

Being an author and passionate youth speaker myself, Elena's ability to get on the level of her young readers leaves me with a sense of awe and profound respect for her writing and speaking abilities.

This book, Blessons For Living "The BEST of BEING" will resonate with parents because it's all about action. It's about demonstrated behavior topics that are significant in the growth of a child like being a friend, being positive and being brave. I usually work with teens and young adults, many of whom have not had strong family units. These teens often miss receiving some of the helpful topics found in this book. In Elena's first book, Blessons for Living, Planting Seeds of Greatness, she speaks about "making good choices" and "loving yourself." These fundamental concepts captured early on can latch onto youth before they become troubled teens. This book aids parents by making these important topics subtle and easy to digest. Young people will take away an understanding of the profound messages in this book.

Elena embodies the image of charisma, genuineness and most of all a love for our next generation. She is self-driven, self-motivated and has a self-assurance that permeates through the reading of her books. I am proud to call Elena a friend and a partner in this journey of giving back to our youth.

Chris Jones has been called one of the most dynamic professional youth speakers in America today. His message challenges teenagers and encourages them to make positive choices in their lives. Chris' message inspires and motivates his audience to action. Whether addressing a room full of disadvantaged youths or adults, Chris' life and personal and professional successes have universal appeal. Chris served as a U.S. Marine Corps Reservist, a U.S. Secret Service Officer (White House Police), and a Maryland County Police Officer. Today, as Co-owner of USA Protection Agency (formerly Jones Executive Security Group) and as the Founder of YDREAM Entrepreneurial Academy for youth and young adults. Chris tells his listeners, "Change Your Thinking and Change Your Life" regardless of your situation.

Blessons For Living
The BEST of BEING

Blesson One: BE A FRIEND   Page 8.

Blesson Two: BE KIND   Page 9.

Blesson Three: BE HELPFUL   Page 11.

Blesson Four: BE GRATEFUL   Page 12.

Blesson Five: BE CURIOUS   Page 13.

Blesson Six: BE POSITIVE   Page 14.

Blesson Seven: BE CAREFUL   Page 15.

Blesson Eight: BE BRAVE   Page 16.

Blesson Nine: BE HAPPY   Page 17.

Blesson Ten: BE YOURSELF   Page 18.

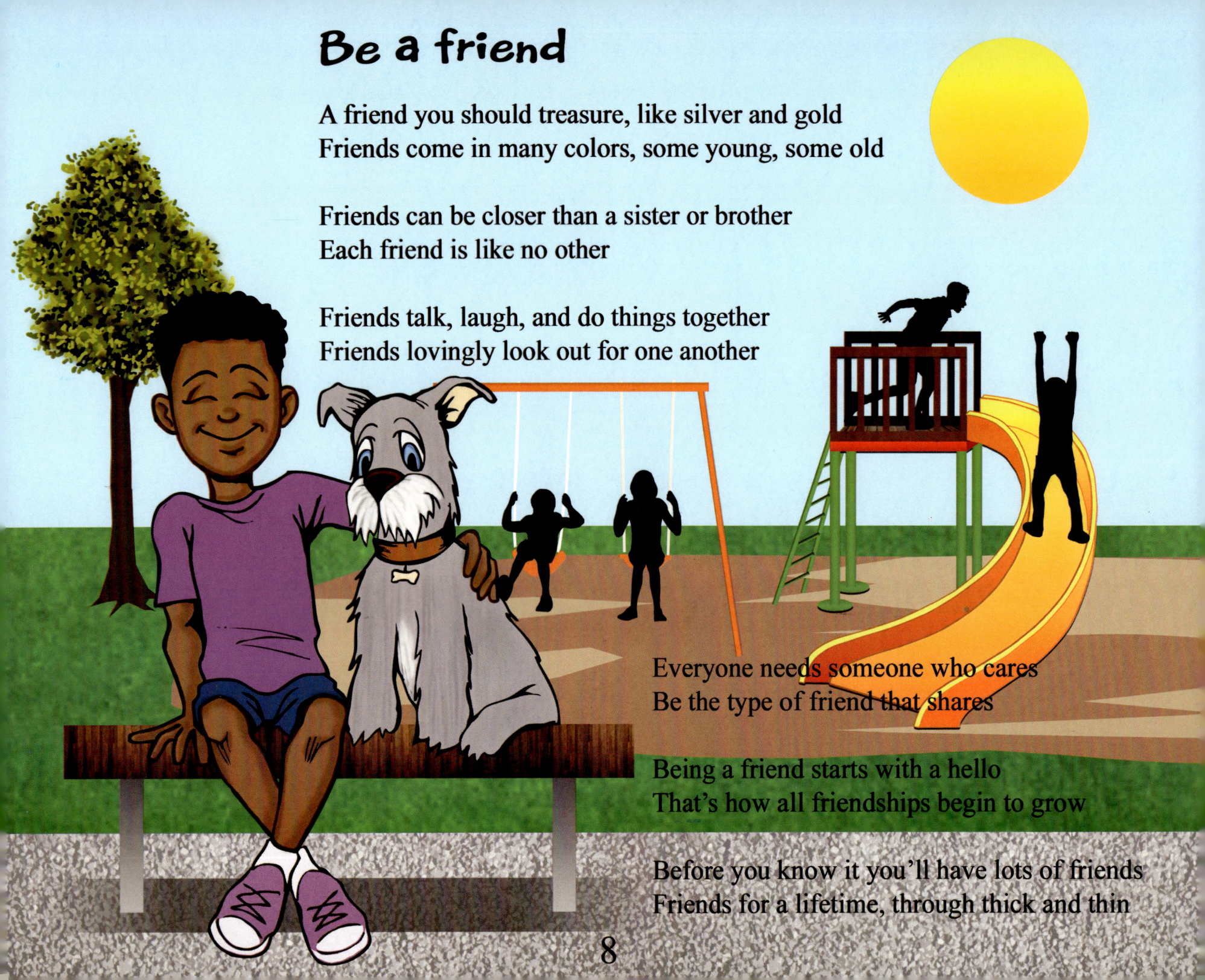

Be a friend

A friend you should treasure, like silver and gold
Friends come in many colors, some young, some old

Friends can be closer than a sister or brother
Each friend is like no other

Friends talk, laugh, and do things together
Friends lovingly look out for one another

Everyone needs someone who cares
Be the type of friend that shares

Being a friend starts with a hello
That's how all friendships begin to grow

Before you know it you'll have lots of friends
Friends for a lifetime, through thick and thin

Be Kind

When you wake up every morning
You must decide to be kind
Being a gift to others
Is something worth your time?

"A smile, a nice greeting, a simple thank you"
Are perfect acts of kindness that you can do

When you are kind you will discover
That it matters that we care for each other

When kindness is an action
All will find satisfaction

When you are kind it makes YOU feel warm inside
Kindness comes from your heart where love resides

A Blesson is a lesson shared.

It's a blessing to share, a blessing to care.

Always remember and never forget.

Blessons flow to help you grow.

Oh what a Blesson it is!

Be Helpful

No matter how small you are
You can be a star

You can be helpful!

Think of what you can do
Or just say "How may I help you?"

Did you know that a smile can make someone's day
Yes, a smile could make sadness go away

Listening is a way to help
People love a listening ear
Give a hug, lend a hand
Let them know a friend is near

Helping can even be fun
You'll feel great when your helpful deed is done

Being helpful is a beautiful trait
One that's necessary for you to be great

Be Grateful

To be grateful is easy
Just appreciate what you see
Beauty is all around you
Just open your eyes and see

We all have things to appreciate
Just count a few with me
A new day, air to breath
Flowers and trees given to us for free

Gratitude is a special place
Where you will also find love and grace

When you are grateful for the smallest things
You'll always see the gifts that every day brings

Be Curious

The world is full of wonder
Like a natural waterfall
Some mountains are massive
Some trees stand amazingly tall

What about a computer
It hasn't always been around
Until someone was curious
Technology was nowhere to be found

Curiosity starts with questions
Who, what, when, where, and why
That's how inventions come to be
Like the plane that lets us fly

Be Positive

Being positive is right
To make your future bright

It begins in the mind
The right choice you will find
Hope for the best
And forget about the rest

Can you imagine if we could only see
Unlimited possibility?

When you believe the best will come
Don't worry where it comes from
Just know good is coming your way
And favor will arrive to stay

It's going to be a great day
"I will make new friends"
Believe the positive words you say
Speak it, think it, so it begins

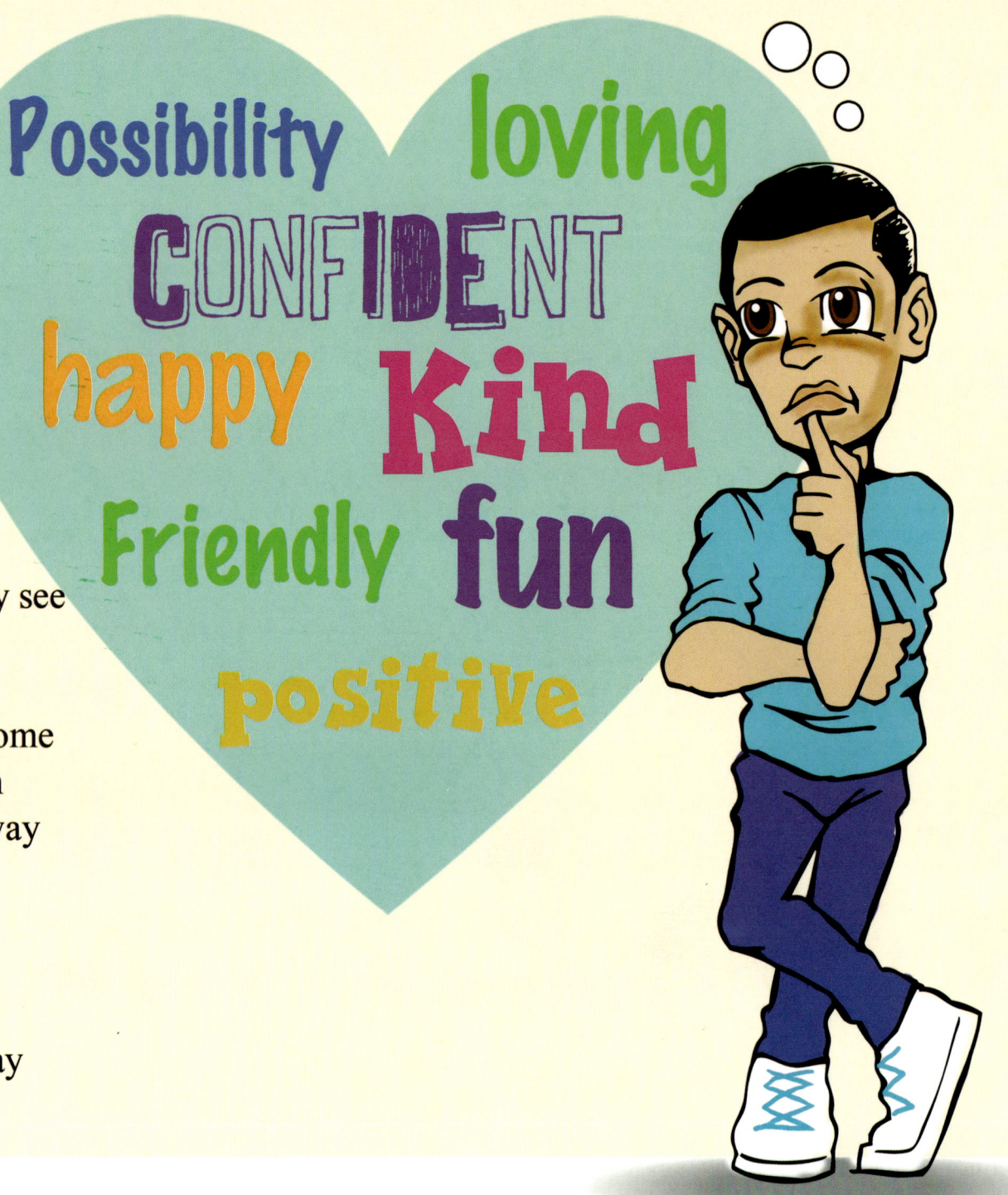

Be Careful

There is a reason for safety
A reason for rules
Be safe on the go
Especially near a pool

Take your time
Don't move too fast
Safety First!!!
Because injuries last

Don't be sneaky
Do what's right
Even when your parents
Are out of sight

You are loved
And special too!
Be careful precious one
Be safe in all you do

Be Brave

Be brave in this world
You don't need to fear
When you enter into it bravely
The way for you is clear

Nothing can stop you
No one can stand in your way
Just make up in your mind
To be brave every day

Whatever your challenge may be
Stand strong, shoulders back
Let the Hero inside of you act

Sometimes you will get scared
All of us do
Face your fears one at a time
And always believe in you

SUPER HEROES ARE REAL

Be Happy

Every day you get to decide
Regardless of the sun or clouds in the sky
What your attitude will be
And wether or not you'll be happy

To be happy is a choice
A good feeling inside
It's a decision you make
To be happy at any time

Happiness is catchy
It's something we'd rather be
Your heart desires that feeling
That's full of energy

One way to be happy
Is to think of all the ways
That you have been blessed
Each and every day

Be Yourself

Here's a fact for you
You are one of a kind
You know what that means
You glow with a special shine

There is only one of you
Every part of you is different
That means you are a gift
You're a beautifully wrapped present

So believe in yourself
Be happy to be you
You were made for a special reason
There something only you can do

You are not only beautiful, you are uniquely you!

A Blesson is a lesson shared.

It can be heard, earned, learned.

But it's always a gift

that gives you a lift.

Oh what a Blesson it is!

For Speaking Engagements, Book Signings, Appearances, and Interviews

Contact:

ELENA M. NEELY

Blessons For Living
P.O. Box 23521
Alexandria, VA 22304

www.blessonsforliving.com

Email
BlessonsForLiving@gmail.com
elenaneely@cs.com

Facebook and Twitter:
@blessons4living

About the Author

Elena Neely is a thoughtful and intentional author, national speaker, motivating mom, teen advisor and owner/publisher of Blessons for Living, LLC which is dedicated to aspiring youth and young adults to manifest a life of greatness. By sharing life's greatest lessons, the Blessons for Living book series is a blessing to generations to come.

About the Illustrator

Los Angeles based visual artist and digital creative service provider, Terry Did'Um Bolen, has been honing his skills as a children's book illustrator for several years. His personal style emanates joy and peace that has captured the hearts of young and mature followers across the world. Terry's true passion is using his gift to inspire children of all ages to dream, stretch out their wings and believe that all things are possible.